FOOTBALL

SCORE WITH STEM!

By K. C. Kelley

Consultant: Tammy Englund, science educator

BEARPORT
PUBLISHING

Minneapolis, Minnesota

Credits

Cover and Title Page, © Mtsaride/Shutterstock; background image, © Vera Larina/Shutterstock; 5, © Focus on Football; 6, © Charlie Neibergall/AP Images; 7, Scott Boehm/AP Images; 8, © David Lee/Shutterstock; 9, © Cooper Neill/AP Images; 9 inset, Wikimedia; 10, © Focus on Football; 11 top, © Steve Cukrov/Shutterstock; 11 bottom, © Focus on Football; 12 top, © Focus on Football; 12 bottom, © Andrey Popov/Shutterstock; 13, © Focus on Football; 14–15, © Focus on Football; 15 left, © Nicky Blade/iStock; 15 right, © Victor Moussa/Shutterstock; 16–17, Courtesy Intel Corp.; 17, Courtesy Intel Corp.; 18–19, © Tom Lynn/MCT/Newscom; 20–21, © Dylan Stewart/Image of Sport/Newscom; 20 inset, © Jevone Moore/Icon Sportswire DMK/Newscom; 22, © enterlinedesign/Shutterstock; 23 top, © Image of Sport/Newscom; 23 bottom, © Happy Vector/iStock; 24, © Focus on Football; 25, © Focus on Football; 26–27, © Focus on Football; 27, © Focus on Football; 28, © Mtsaride/Shutterstock; 31, © CapturePB/Shutterstock

Bearport Publishing Company
Minneapolis, Minnesota
President: Jen Jenson
Director of Product Development: Spencer Brinker
Senior Editor: Allison Juda
Associate Editor: Charly Haley
Designer: Colin O'Dea

Produced by Shoreline Publishing Group LLC
Santa Barbara, California
Designer: Patty Kelley
Editorial Director: James Buckley Jr.

Library of Congress Cataloging-in-Publication Data

Names: Kelley, K. C., author.
Title: Football : score with STEM! / by K.C. Kelley.
Description: Minneapolis, Minnesota : Bearport Publishing Company, 2022. |
    Series: Sports STEM | Includes bibliographical references and index.
Identifiers: LCCN 2021001066 (print) | LCCN 2021001067 (ebook) | ISBN
    9781636911755 (library binding) | ISBN 9781636911823 (paperback) | ISBN
    9781636911892 (ebook)
Subjects: LCSH: Football--Juvenile literature. | Sports sciences--Juvenile
    literature.
Classification: LCC GV950.7 .K439 2022 (print) | LCC GV950.7 (ebook) |
    DDC 796.33--dc23
LC record available at https://lccn.loc.gov/2021001066
LC ebook record available at https://lccn.loc.gov/2021001067

For more information, write to Bearport Publishing, 5357 Penn Avenue South, Minneapolis, MN 55419. Printed in the United States of America.

Contents

Football and STEM

The Kansas City Chiefs trail by four points late in their National Football League (NFL) game. Quarterback Patrick Mahomes drops back to pass. He spots an open receiver. Mahomes calls on all of his training—and on STEM—to make the play.

He throws the ball in a high **arc** down the field. The spinning football cuts through the air in a perfect **spiral**. A speedy receiver tracks the path of the pass. He times his speed to meet the ball as it comes down, right into his hands! Touchdown!

SCIENCE: From long passes to soaring field goals, a football moves according to the rules of physics.

TECHNOLOGY: Discover how wearable tech and digital recordings tell us more about the game.

ENGINEERING: Modern stadiums are designed to help fans enjoy games in new and exciting ways.

MATH: Information about teams and players is gathered as numbers called **stats**. A winning score is just the beginning!

Patrick Mahomes throws a pass for the Kansas City Chiefs.

Big Bodies!

Several large players line up and stand tall to protect their quarterback. Together, these players weigh more than 1,550 pounds (703 kg)! All that bulk keeps the QB safe from tacklers and gives him time to throw. Touchdown! The quarterback was protected by big and strong teammates. How did the players get so large?

Size and strength help offensive linemen protect their QB.

Getting Big with Biology

Many linemen are bound to be big from the start. A lot about our bodies comes from what we inherit from our parents.

Food provides the energy for bodies to grow even bigger. Players need to eat the right mix of carbohydrates for fuel, **protein** to build and repair muscles, and only a little bit of fat.

Football Physics

The holder sets the football onto the field just before the kicker smashes his foot into the ball. The ball flies up over the blockers and through the **uprights**. Three points and another win for science!

Up and over the crossbar for three points!

Force in Football

Scientists know that movement relates directly to **force**. In this case, the force comes from the kicker's foot swinging toward the ball sitting on the ground. That force is then transferred to the ball, causing it to fly into the air. This action follows a law of motion—objects at rest stay that way until a force acts on them. That ball won't fly by itself!

Kickers put physics into action.

English scientist Sir Isaac Newton is known for three laws of motion. These laws describe the relationship of objects to forces acting on them and the movement caused by those forces. His third law describes the action and reaction forces that make football possible!

The Right Way to Pass

The star quarterback runs to the right. He sees an open receiver down the field and fires a pass to his teammate. But the ball wobbles in the air. The QB's throw was off! Back in the huddle, the quarterback thinks about his next pass. How can he make sure it will be on target?

Spinning the ball will help get a pass where it is supposed to go.

Spiral for Success

It's time for the quarterback to use science. On his next throw, the ball moves in a perfect spiral. The ball spins around a central **axis** as it leaves his fingers. A ball that spirals creates less resistance and moves through the air more easily. The football follows a smooth arc and lands in the receiver's hands. Touchdown!

Footballs are designed to help players throw spirals. By placing some fingers on the laces, a player can spin the ball on its release. Without the laces to grab, throwing a spiral would be much harder!

Finding the Right Players

The tall receiver leaps high above the defense to grab the pass. Now, it's time to run! Receivers who can pile up the most yards after a catch really help their teams. But how do pro teams know which receivers—and other players—to choose?

Using Data

A tech company works with the NFL to gather **data** about players. **Sensors** are placed inside players' shoulder pads to gather information about how they play. This data includes how far and fast receivers can run from defenders. The company then creates a stat called expected yards after catch. Seeing a young player's stats can reveal a star in the making.

Sensors in shoulder pads beam out information.

Head Protection

Believe it or not, football players in the late 1800s and early 1900s did not wear helmets! The first helmets in the 1930s were made from leather and had no face protection. Even in the 1960s, when hard plastic helmets became **mandatory**, players still got hurt. The latest technology makes today's helmets safer than ever.

All NFL players must wear helmets.

Distribution of Force

When a player is hit, the force of the impact transfers energy. A safe helmet reduces the amount of energy that reaches a player's head. Hard plastic on the outside of a helmet and foam padding on the inside work together to spread the energy around so it doesn't hit only one point. The padding inside also helps absorb some of the energy before it reaches the head.

The plastic shell and padding spread the force of impact.

Leather helmets didn't do much to protect against hard hits.

Catching All the Action

With the snap, both teams spring into action. The quarterback drops back to pass. His linemen block as defenders rush in. Receivers sprint down the field, and defensive backs race to cover them. With everything happening so fast, how can you see it all?

Cameras peer down at the action.

A View from Every Angle

New video technology called True View is helping NFL fans see plays from every angle. The system captures video and photos from dozens of cameras positioned around the field. A computer then combines the separate images into one continuous view. It's a great way to see all of the action that goes into a successful play.

Cameras help fans get a full view of the field.

One type of True View video even lets fans see what it's like to score a touchdown. The video looks as if you are seeing out of a player's face mask. The camera turns like the player's head to show a tackle nearby or the goal line straight ahead!

17

Warming the Field

Football games are played in all kinds of weather. Even when the snow is falling and a chilly wind is blowing, the game must go on! In some stadiums, fans shiver in their seats, but the players aren't running and tackling on a hard, icy ground. Thanks to smart engineering, games in freezing weather can be played on soft green grass!

The Secret Is Underground

Stadiums built in places with cold weather often have a secret buried under their turf. A grid of plastic pipes hides beneath the grass and dirt. Pumps push a hot water mixture through the pipes. The warmth keeps the grass and dirt above from freezing. This makes a safer—and more comfortable—playing field.

More than 43 miles (69.2 km) of pipes are buried under Lambeau Field, home of the Green Bay Packers.

Building the Biggest Field

In 2020, the NFL's Los Angeles Rams and Los Angeles Chargers moved into SoFi Stadium, the largest stadium in the world. The high-tech building cost $5 billion to build and has room for 100,000 fans. The structure is so large that engineers wanted to be sure airplanes from the nearby Los Angeles airport had enough room to fly over. So, they dug down and built the stadium almost 100 feet (30 m) into the ground.

Look Up . . . and Out!

SoFi's enormous ceiling is made with see-through panels of strong plastic so fans can enjoy the sunny California weather. Engineers also wanted fans to feel the breeze. The stadium's huge side and roof panels can open to let in fresh air.

Large openings at either end of SoFi Stadium allow breezes to flow over fans and players.

SoFi's ring-shaped video screen is 120 yards (110 m) long. That's longer than the field! Engineers created a special cable system to hold up the screen, which weighs more than 2 million lbs (900,000 kg). The screen can show videos and photos to fans all around the stadium.

Math in Action

It's **first down** and 10 yards to go. An offensive receiver catches the ball and then runs up the field. The other team's defense tackles him after a gain of six yards. It's time for the offense to choose their next play with a little help from math.

10 YARDS

Orange poles and a 10-yard chain help teams and officials measure 10 yards.

Down and Distance

When a football team gets the ball for a first down, they must move the ball at least 10 yards within four plays to get another first down and keep the ball. When the receiver was tackled on first down, he had run six yards. The team needed to gain at least four more yards to earn another first down.

Officials sometimes bring the chain onto the field to see if a team has advanced 10 yards.

Scoring Points

Here is how football teams fill up the scoreboard with points.

Touchdown (TD)	6 points
Kick after a TD	1 point
Short pass or run after a TD	2 points
Defensive safety	2 points
Field goal	3 points

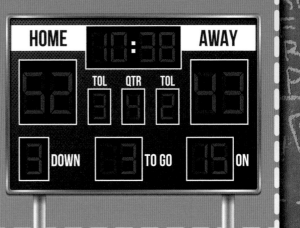

HOME 10:38 AWAY

52 TOL 3 QTR 8 TOL 2 43

3 DOWN 33 TO GO 15 ON

Measuring Success

Late in the game, a running back has 95 rushing yards. He takes the **handoff** and sprints around the end. He then races 11 yards before he is tackled. The run gives him a total of 106 rushing yards in the game—a big achievement in football!

Running plays often start with a handoff.

Per-Game Averages

A per-game average is a number that helps show how good a player is throughout a season. To calculate this stat, divide the total number of rushing yards by the total number of games played. A player who ran 675 yards in 6 games has a per-game average of 112.5 yards.

675 yards ÷ 6 games = 112.5 yards per game (YPG)

Derrick Henry averaged 126.7 yards per game in the 2020 NFL season. That was the best in the league.

The GOAT

There is always debate about who is the greatest quarterback of all time. But how do you decide who is the GOAT? Is it the player who completes the most passes? What about the quarterback with the most touchdown passes? Or is it simply the QB who leads his team to the most victories?

Aaron Rodgers has led the NFL in passer rating three times. Is he the GOAT?

Passer Rating

The NFL created a special **formula** to help you get one step closer to finding your GOAT. The formula combines several stats, including touchdown passes, yards gained, and **interception** rates. The numbers are entered into the formula, and the result is called the passer rating. A perfect passer rating is 158.3, and all the best NFL passers have ratings above 90.

Patrick Mahomes has the best career passer rating of any player. He had a rating of 108.7 through 2020. The best rating for a single season was 122.5 by Rodgers in 2011. Which do you think is more impressive?

Do the Math!

It's time to do some football math! Learn how to calculate three types of football stats. Then, find out which players and teams had the best stats.

Adding Yards from Scrimmage

Running backs gain yards from **scrimmage** by running the ball for rushing yards and by catching passes for receiving yards. Add the yards for each player below to find their total.

1. Which player had more yards from scrimmage?

PLAYER	RUSHING YARDS	RECEIVING YARDS
Nick Chubb	1,494	278
Dalvin Cook	1,135	519

Passing and Field Goal Percentages

A percentage is a part of a whole number expressed in hundredths. To find each percentage, divide the number of times a player succeeded by his number of attempts, and then move the decimal point two places to the right.

2. Which quarterback had the higher pass completion percentage?

PLAYER	PASS COMPLETIONS	PASS ATTEMPTS
Drew Brees	281	378
Derek Carr	361	513
Jared Goff	394	626

3. Which kicker had the higher field goal percentage?

PLAYER	FIELD GOALS MADE	FIELD GOALS ATTEMPTED
Chris Boswell	29	31
Mason Crosby	22	24

Per-Game Averages

To find an average per game, divide the total of something by the number of games played.

4. Rushing yards show how far a runner went while carrying the ball. Which player had the better per-game average for rushing yards?

PLAYER	TOTAL RUSHING YARDS	GAMES PLAYED
Jim Brown	12,312	118
Barry Sanders	15,269	153

5. Teams pile up stats, too. Which of these teams had the higher average of sacks per game?

TEAM	TOTAL SACKS	GAMES PLAYED
Pittsburgh Steelers	45	16
New Orleans Saints	47	18

Answers:
1. Chubb had a total of 1,772 yards from scrimmage, while Cook had 1,654. Chubb had more yards from scrimmage.
2. Brees completed 74.3 percent of his passes. Carr was close behind at 70.4 percent completed. Goff trailed behind at 62.9 percent.
3. Boswell's field goal percentage of 93.5 was higher than Crosby's 91.7.
4. Brown's career per-game average for rushing yards was 104.3, the highest of all time. Sanders is second-best with 99.8 yards per game.
5. The Saints had more total sacks, but the Steelers's per-game average was higher, 2.81 to 2.61.

Glossary

arc a path that follows a curve

axis an imaginary line around which something happens

data information often in the form of numbers

first down the beginning of a series of offensive plays

force the push or pull of an object

formula a series of steps needed to solve a math problem

handoff a play in which the quarterback places the ball right into the hands of another player

interception a pass caught by the opposing team

mandatory required

protein a substance in food that is needed for the human body's muscles to work and grow

scrimmage short for line of scrimmage; the point on the field from which a play begin

sensors devices that detect and gather information

spiral the spin of a football it moves through the air afte being thrown

stats short for statistics; information stated as numbe

uprights the tall posts at ea end of a football field

Read More

George, Enzo. *Physical Science in Football (Science Gets Physical).* New York: Crabtree Publishing Company, 2020.

Havelka, Jacqueline. *STEM in Football (Connecting STEM and Sports).* Philadelphia: Mason Crest, 2020.

McCollum, Sean. *Full STEAM Football: Science, Technology, Engineering, Arts, and Mathematics of the Game (Full STEAM Sports).* North Mankato, MN: Capstone Press, 2019.

Learn More Online

1. Go to **www.factsurfer.com**

2. Enter "**STEM Football**" into the search box.

3. Click on the cover of this book to see a list of websites.

Index

About the Author

K. C. Kelley has written more than 100 books on sports for young readers, including titles on basketball, soccer, baseball, the Olympics, and much more. He used to work for *Sports Illustrated* and the National Football League.